PHILIPPIANS

JESUS OUR JOY

DONALD BAKER

9 STUDIES
FOR INDIVIDUALS
OR GROUPS

Life
Builder
Study

INTER-VARSITY PRESS
36 Causton Street, London SW1P 4ST, England
Email: ivp@ivpbooks.com
Website: www.ivpbooks.com

Originally published in the United States of America in the LifeGuide® Bible Studies series in 1985 by InterVarsity Press, Downers Grove, Illinois
Second edition published 1999
First published in Great Britain by Scripture Union in 2000
This edition published in Great Britain by Inter-Varsity Press 2018

British Library Cataloguing-in-Publication Data
A catalogue record for this book is available from the British Library.

ISBN: 978–1–78359–804–5

Printed in Great Britain by Ashford Colour Press Ltd, Gosport, Hampshire

Inter-Varsity Press publishes Christian books that are true to the Bible and that communicate the gospel, develop discipleship and strengthen the church for its mission in the world.

IVP originated within the Inter-Varsity Fellowship, now the Universities and Colleges Christian Fellowship, a student movement connecting Christian Unions in universities and colleges throughout Great Britain, and a member movement of the International Fellowship of Evangelical Students. Website: www.uccf.org.uk. That historic association is maintained, and all senior IVP staff and committee members subscribe to the UCCF Basis of Faith.

Contents

Getting the Most Out of *Philippians*

"Rejoice in the Lord always," the author of Philippians exhorts us, "I will say it again: Rejoice!" Coming from most people, such words might sound trite and simplistic, but this is the apostle Paul speaking, a man who was not writing from a padded–leather office chair surrounded by books on how to be happy. On the contrary, he was a prisoner awaiting news that could result in his death. It isn't hard to get behind the words of Philippians and see the tension and uncertainty. Yet through it all we see a man whose life is filled with joy.

As we study Philippians, we discover Paul's secret: that a life lived for the glory of God will overflow with joy. What a message for our hurting world!

Philippi was an important city because it straddled the great east-west highway known as the Egnatian Way. The population of this city was cosmopolitan, being made up of Tracians, Greeks, Romans and a few Jews. In the center of the city was a large forum surrounded by temples, a library, fountains, monuments and public baths.

In 42 B.C. Antony and Octavian defeated Brutus and Cassius near Philippi. In honor of his victory Antony made Philippi a Roman colony. This provided the Philippians with special rights and privileges as Roman citizens, and they responded with a great deal of pride and loyalty. Women enjoyed a high status in Philippi—taking an active part in both public and business life. Because of this, women also had important responsibilities in the Philippian church.

Paul founded this church sometime around the year A.D. 50, during his second missionary journey (Acts 16:12–40). From the letter to the Philippians, we learn that this church was taking its share of suffering (1:29); it was in some danger of division (1:27; 2:2; 4:2), it may have been leaning toward a doctrine of perfectionism (3:12–13), and it was threatened by the teaching of Judaizers—a group which insisted that all Christians adhere to Jewish laws and customs. Despite these problems Paul's love for this church was obvious. He sincerely rejoiced at the progress they were making.

We know that Paul was writing to the Philippians from prison (1:12–14). Unfortunately, it is not clear which prison he was writing from. If he was writing during his imprisonment in Rome, then the letter can be dated sometime between A.D. 61–63. However, many scholars have pointed out that the conditions that Paul describes seem much harsher than what we know of the Roman imprisonment (Acts 28:16, 30–31). It could be that there was an earlier imprisonment not recorded in Acts. A good case has been made for Ephesus. If this is true, Philippians would have been written about A.D. 54.

Paul had several reasons for writing this letter. He wanted to explain why he was sending a man named Epaphroditus back to Philippi. He also wanted to thank the Philippians for the gift of money they had sent and to reassure his friends of his condition. Also the news Paul had received concerning the Philippians made him long to encourage and advise a church he loved.

May you learn to apply Paul's secret to joyful living as you study this warm and encouraging letter.

Suggestions for Individual Study

1. As you begin each study, pray that God will speak to you through his Word.

2. Read the introduction to the study and respond to the "personal reflection" question or exercise. This is designed to help you focus on God and on the theme of the study.

3. Each study deals with a particular passage, so that you can delve into the author's meaning in that context. Read and reread the passage to be studied. If you are studying a book, it will be helpful to read through the entire book prior to the first study. The questions are written using the language of the New International Version, so you may wish to use that version of the Bible. The New Revised Standard

Version is also recommended.

4. This is an inductive Bible study, designed to help you discover for yourself what Scripture is saying. The study includes three types of questions. *Observation* questions ask about the basic facts: who, what, when, where and how. *Interpretation* questions delve into the meaning of the passage. *Application* questions help you discover the implications of the text for growing in Christ. These three keys unlock the treasures of Scripture.

Write your answers to the questions in the spaces provided or in a personal journal. Writing can bring clarity and deeper understanding of yourself and of God's Word.

5. It might be good to have a Bible dictionary handy. Use it to look up any unfamiliar words, names or places.

6. Use the prayer suggestion to guide you in thanking God for what you have learned and to pray about the applications that have come to mind.

7. You may want to go on to the suggestion under "Now or Later," or you may want to use that idea for your next study.

Suggestions for Members of a Group Study

1. Come to the study prepared. Follow the suggestions for individual study mentioned above. You will find that careful preparation will greatly enrich your time spent in group discussion.

2. Be willing to participate in the discussion. The leader of your group will not be lecturing. Instead, he or she will be encouraging the members of the group to discuss what they have learned. The leader will be asking the questions that are found in this guide.

3. Stick to the topic being discussed. Your answers should be based on the verses that are the focus of the discussion and not on outside authorities such as commentaries or speakers. These studies focus on a particular passage of Scripture. Only rarely should you refer to other portions of the Bible. This allows for everyone to participate in in-depth study on equal ground.

4. Be sensitive to the other members of the group. Listen attentively when they describe what they have learned. You may be surprised by their insights! Each question assumes a variety of answers. Many questions do not have "right" answers, particularly questions that aim at meaning or application. Instead the questions push us to explore the passage more thoroughly.

   When possible, link what you say to the comments of others. Also be affirming whenever you can. This will encourage some of the more hesitant members of the group to participate.

5. Be careful not to dominate the discussion. We are sometimes so eager to express our thoughts that we leave little opportunity for others to respond. By all means participate! But allow others to do so too.

6. Expect God to teach you through the passage being discussed and through the other members of the group. Pray that you will have an enjoyable and profitable time together, but also that as a result of the study, you will find ways that you can take action individually and/ or as a group.

7. Remember that anything said in the group is considered confidential and should not be discussed outside the group unless specific permission is given to do so.

8. If you are the group leader, you will find additional suggestions at the back of the guide.

1

The God Who Pursues Us

Acts 16:6–34

An anonymous poet in the nineteenth century penned these words that have become a hymn:

> I sought the Lord, and afterward I knew
> He moved my soul to seek Him, seeking me;
> It was not I that found, O Saviour true;
> No, I was found of Thee.

GROUP DISCUSSION. What do you remember about your earliest encounter with God? Did you pursue God, or did he pursue you?

PERSONAL REFLECTION. In what ways was God active in your life even before you responded to him?

Paul writes to the Philippians that he is "confident of this, that he who began a good work in you will carry it on to completion until the day of Christ Jesus" (Philippians 1:6). In this study we will discover how God began the good work in Philippi. *Read Acts 16:6–34.*

1. If you had been travelling with Paul, what evidence would have convinced you that you were obeying the will of God?

_____

2. What do verses 6–12 reveal about the way God guided these missionaries to Philippi?

_____

3. In verses 13–15 God leads the missionaries to Lydia, the first Christian convert. Compare the way God leads here to the way in which he first led them to Macedonia.

_____

4. What does this teach you about the methods God may use to speak to you?

_____

5. Imagine that you had been present during the events described in verses 16–18. How would they have affected your view of these missionaries and Jesus Christ?

6. Why do you suppose the owners of the slave girl were unable to see God at work?

7. What attitudes and personal agendas have prevented you from seeing God at work?

8. Imagine that you are imprisoned with Paul and Silas (vv. 22–24). What sights, sounds, smells and emotions would you be experiencing?

9. What do you think enabled Paul and Silas to sing at a time like this (v. 25)?

10. How did God use circumstances in order to claim the jailer for himself?

11. How has God controlled the people and events surrounding your life in order to speak to you?

Thank God for the specific people and circumstances he used to move you toward himself.

Now or Later

12. This passage is a beautiful example of how the Spirit of God and the servants of God work together in evangelism. What specific principles of evangelism can you learn from this passage?

13. How should these principles affect your witness?

2

An Encouraging Example

Philippians 1 : 1–11

Have you ever listened while others prayed for you? If so, you know how great it feels to be assured that others care. Giving affirmation to friends can encourage holiness and spiritual growth.

GROUP DISCUSSION. As a group take time to tell each person in the group what character qualities you have observed in them and what you appreciate about them. Continue until each member of the group has been affirmed in this way.

PERSONAL REFLECTION. How does affirmation help you to become a better person?

Paul began many of his letters with a prayer of thanksgiving, but this letter begins with a prayer of unusually great warmth and affirmation. As you read this passage, imagine yourself sitting with Lydia, the slave girl and the jailer as this letter is opened and read for the first time. *Read Philippians 1:1–11.*

1. How would you have felt if you were among the Philippian Christians the first time this letter was read?

2. From verses 3–8 describe Paul's feelings toward the Philippians.

Why does he feel this way about them?

3. What causes Paul to be so confident about the Philippians' future (v. 6)?

4. Where do you see God continuing his "good work" in your life or in your Christian community?

5. What do verses 3–8 reveal about healthy Christian relationships?

6. In what relationships have you experienced the kind of partnership that Paul describes here?

What can be done to strengthen these relationships?

_____

7. What are Paul's prayer requests for the Philippians (vv. 9–11)?

_____

8. Why would each of these qualities be essential to spiritual maturity?

_____

9. "Encouragement is the kind of expression that helps someone want to be a better Christian, even when life is rough."* According to this definition, how would these verses have encouraged the Philippians?

_____

*Larry Crabb and Dan Allender, *Encouragement* (Zondervan, 1984), p. 10.

10. What can you do through words, prayers and actions to encourage someone today?

Using Paul's prayer as a model, spend a few minutes thanking God and praying for someone you love in Christ.

Now or Later

Compare and contrast Philippians 1:3–11 with Colossians 1:3–14. What additional insights can you find to help you encourage others?

3

Joy in the Worst of Times

Philippians 1:12–30

There is nothing that will test our beliefs more than suffering for them.

GROUP DISCUSSION. Throughout history people have given their lives for such things as God, country, family, ideals, friends, love, science, adventure or compassion. For which of these would you be willing to die? What issues are involved in forming your answer?

PERSONAL REFLECTION. When has it been most difficult for you to have hope in the Lord?

In this passage we discover that Paul is writing to the Philippians from prison. This puts a whole new perspective on the joyful mood of the letter. While Paul is writing, he is experiencing what most of us would describe as awful circumstances. Yet even at a time like this, Paul's first concern is that Christ is praised. This passage can teach us how to honor Christ in a difficult situation. *Read Philippians 1:12–30.*

1. What things have happened to Paul that you would find discouraging?

2. Why isn't Paul upset by his imprisonment (vv. 12–14)?

3. Compare the motives of the two groups described in verses 15–18.

4. What does Paul mean when he asks, "What does it matter?" in verse 18?

5. When have you been critical of the motives or methods of other Christians?

What advice would Paul give to you about this?

6. What are Paul's considerations in choosing between life and death (vv. 20–26)?

7. What does Paul's statement "For to me, to live is Christ and to die is gain" (v. 21) teach you about living a life of purpose?

8. What does it mean to conduct ourselves in a manner worthy of the gospel (vv. 27–30)?

9. Why is each of these attitudes or actions important, especially in the midst of suffering or persecution?

10. Look back over the passage. Summarize the various factors which can transform difficult circumstances into a joyful, Christ-exalting situation.

11. What are the most difficult circumstances you are presently facing?

How can Christ be exalted in that situation?

Pray that Christ will be honored in the difficult circumstances you face. Pray also for Christians around the world who are being persecuted for their faith.

Now or Later

Study Romans 8:17–30 to learn more of Paul's attitude toward suffering.

4

The Path of
Humility

We speak often of what we deserve to get in life. The idea that we should be rewarded for our actions is ingrained in Western culture. More than any other person who has lived, Jesus Christ deserved to be glorified, but was willing to be treated as a servant.

GROUP DISCUSSION. How would your life be different if Christ had not come? As each member of the group takes a turn at answering this question, think especially about such areas as purpose, motivation, relationships, behavior and desires.

PERSONAL REFLECTION. In what ways has Christ been your servant?

In this study Paul asks us to imitate Christ in his humility by taking on the attitude of a servant. *Read Philippians 2:1–18.*

1. If you had been in Christ's position, what would you have found most demeaning about serving humans?

2. How does Paul define humility in verses 1–4?

3. What does Paul mean when he says that Jesus "did not consider equality with God something to be grasped" (v. 6)?

4. How would Christ's mission have been different if he had grasped for equality?

5. In what areas of your life are you most tempted to seek honor and selfish ambition?

How does Christ's example teach you to respond to these temptations?

---

6. In your own words describe God's response to Jesus' humility (vv. 9–11).

What does this teach about their relationship?

---

7. What motivation does Paul give you in this passage for living a life of service?

---

8. In verses 12–13 Paul says you are to "work out your salvation" because God "works in you." How are these ideas related?

---

9. How are we to be different from the "crooked and depraved generation" in which we live (vv. 14–16)?

10. Paul admits that he hopes to boast when Christ returns (v. 16). Why isn't this conceit?

---

11. How is Paul himself an example of the principles described in this passage (vv. 16–18)?

---

12. What opportunities will you have for humble service during the next few days?

Pray about both the ways you are tempted to be conceited and the opportunities you have to serve.

Now or Later

Read John 13:12–17. If you are in a group, using a basin of water and a towel, take turns washing each other's feet.

If you are not in a group, reflect on ways that we can serve each other similarly today. Put one of these ideas into practice.

5

Servants
of Christ

Philippians 2:19–30

A grade-school teacher who praised your writing; a Sunday school teacher who prompted you to read the Bible on your own; a coach who gave you confidence in your athletic ability: each of us has been shaped and influenced by the examples of teachers, coaches, friends, pastors and mentors.

GROUP DISCUSSION. On a sheet of paper draw a picture that represents the most unforgettable Christian you have met. Take time for each artist to describe his or her drawing.

PERSONAL REFLECTION. What other Christians have been influential in your life?

When the Philippians heard that Paul was in prison, they sent one of their members—a man named Epaphroditus—to Paul with a gift of money. It was his job to help Paul in any way necessary. Epaphroditus returned home carrying the letter to the Philippians. In this section of the letter Paul outlines his future plans and explains why he is sending

Epaphroditus back. The passage gives several beautiful examples of Christian service as displayed in the lives of Timothy, Epaphroditus, Paul and the Philippians. *Read Philippians 2:19–30.*

---

1. Which of the godly men mentioned in these verses would you most like to meet: Paul, Timothy or Epaphroditus?

What would you talk about?

---

2. How is Timothy an example of the Christlike attitude considered in the previous study (vv. 19–23)?

---

3. Why do you think people like Timothy are so rare (v. 20)?

---

4. Imagine that Timothy is being sent to visit your church or fellowship group. What might he do to help you?

5. Since Timothy won't be coming to visit, what are some practical ways you could follow his example?

6. Why is Paul sending Epaphroditus back to Philippi (vv. 25–28)?

7. How is Christ's attitude evident in the relationships among Paul, Epaphroditus and the Philippians (vv. 25–30)?

8. Why is it important to honor people like Epaphroditus?

9. How can you honor the unforgettable Christians you described at the beginning of this study?

10. Examine your plans and goals during the coming week. How can you bring your own interests into closer harmony with those of Jesus Christ?

_____

11. What are some practical ways you can serve those around you during the coming week?

Thank God for those who have been a godly example in your life. Pray that Christ will continue to give you the heart of a servant.

Now or Later

Make plans to honor a pastor, teacher or leader who has unselfishly served you.

6

Rejoice in the Lord

Philippians 3:1–11

St. John of the Cross declared, "The well-known joy of a Christian is not a denial of tears, but an affirmation of that which is deeper than tears."

GROUP DISCUSSION. Describe the most joyful day of your life. What made it so joyful?

PERSONAL REFLECTION. What factors under your control prevent all your days from being joyful?

In these verses Paul contrasts his old life of misery with his new life of rejoicing, and he invites us to join him in joy. *Read Philippians 3:1–11.*

1. What has Paul found that brings joy, and what has he found that destroys joy?

2. What would the old Paul (vv. 4–6) have been like as a friend?

3. Why is Paul so stern in his warning against the kind of person he used to be (vv. 2–3)?

4. If friends were to write references for your résumé, what would they say to convince prospective employers that you are a good person?

5. Why does Paul consider his resume (and yours) to be "rubbish" (v. 8)?

6. In verse 6 Paul speaks of "legalistic righteousness." What legalisms are today's Christians pressured to keep?

7. How do these legalisms get in the way of knowing Christ and rejoicing in the Lord?

8. How does the new Paul (vv. 7–11) differ from the old?

How have his reasons for confidence changed?

9. What are Paul's goals in life?

10. How are suffering and death involved in helping us to know Christ (v. 10)?

11. How has following Christ been costly for you?

How have your sacrifices produced joy in your life?

Pray that you may experience a life of joy that is derived from a right relationship with Jesus Christ.

Now or Later

Paul uses the words *joy* and *rejoice* many times in Philippians. Read Philippians 1:4, 18; 2:2, 17; 3:1; 4:1, 4, 10 looking for Paul's reasons for joy. What additional reasons can you find to rejoice?

7

Onward to
the Goal

Philippians 3:12–4:1

The primary goals in your life can be identified by the things you dream about, plan for, work for, save for and aim for.

GROUP DISCUSSION. What have been your two or three primary goals, and what have you done to achieve them?

PERSONAL REFLECTION. If someone had been observing you during the past week, what would they conclude were your primary goals?

Paul uses the language of an athlete preparing for the biggest race of his life as he describes his dedication to reaching heaven. In this study Paul will act as our coach, challenging us to his high level of devotion to spiritual goals. *Read Philippians 3:12–4:1.*

1. Describe the people you think Paul had in mind as he wrote.

2. Paul compares his quest for heaven to a race. What are the similarities?

_____

3. How can looking back distract us from running the Christian race (v. 13)?

_____

4. What is behind you that you need to forget in order to strain toward the things ahead?

_____

5. What are you presently doing that could be described as "straining toward heaven"?

_____

6. Why is Paul so confident about his views (vv. 15–16)?

_____

7. How does God make our errors clear to us?

_____

8. In verses 17–21 Paul contrasts the game plan of Christians with "enemies of the cross." What are the differences in goals and destiny?

9. What lesser goals have sidetracked you from working toward your real purpose?

10. In verse 17 Paul is like a coach calling his team to follow his example. Summarize the tips the coach has given us in this passage.

11. In what specific ways can you begin to follow Paul's example more fully?

Pray that God will help you to focus on the heavenly goal and not be sidetracked by temptations.

Now or Later

Read Matthew 13:44–46. Why are the people in these parables so willing to sell all that they have?

In what ways is Paul like the pearl merchant?

What might you have to sell in order to gain the pearl?

8

Stress-free Living

Philippians 4:2–9

Stress has been identified as one of the great killers of our day. It causes physical problems such as high blood pressure, headaches and ulcers, as well as emotional problems like depression, irritability and burnout.

GROUP DISCUSSION. Draw a graph showing the levels of stress in your life from birth until the present. Share your graph with your group and tell how the periods of greatest stress have affected you.

PERSONAL REFLECTION. What has your experience of God been like during your times of greatest stress?

Paul was living with many powerful stressors (he was in prison, facing possible execution while defending himself against critics and heretics inside the church), yet he seemed to be strangely at peace. In this study Paul reveals some of the secrets of his peace. *Read Philippians 4:2–9.*

1. What were some of the factors causing stress in the Philippian church?

Which of these has caused stress in your relationships? How?

_____

2. In verse 2 Paul pleads with Euodia and Syntyche "to agree with each other in the Lord." What effect do you think their broken relationship was having on the rest of the church?

_____

3. What might a "loyal yokefellow" do to help these women (v. 3)?

_____

4. What should be your response to disagreements within your church or fellowship group?

5. How can rejoicing help to defuse a stressful situation (v. 4)?

6. How can gentleness be made "evident to all" (v. 5)?

7. What should be the role of prayer in our lives (vv. 6–7)?

8. What results of prayer does Paul promise?

9. How can true, noble, right, pure, lovely, admirable, excellent and praiseworthy thoughts help cleanse our minds and restore our tranquility (v. 8)?

10. What helps you to control your thoughts?

11. In verse 9 Paul tells us that the God of peace will be with us as we practice what we have learned. What have you learned in this passage that you need to put into practice?

Pray that God will teach you to control the stressors that rob you of his joy.

Now or Later

Read James 4:1–12. What alternatives to fighting and quarreling does James suggest?

Using James's counsel, formulate the advice you would offer to Euodia and Syntyche if you were in the role of "loyal yokefellow."

How can your advice to Euodia and Syntyche be applied to your own life?

9

A Guide
for Giving

Philippians 4:10–23

Giving is a privilege of every Christian, no matter how much we have. Making biblical choices in our giving is a big responsibility that can bring great joy into our lives.

GROUP DISCUSSION. If you had a million dollars to use for God's work, how would you spend it? Why would you choose to spend it in this way?

PERSONAL REFLECTION. How have you grown as a steward of the resources God has given you?

Thank you notes usually include rather conventional phrases about the thankfulness of the recipient and the thoughtfulness of the giver. In Philippians 4 Paul thanks the Philippians for a gift of money they sent. However, it is a most unusual thank you note. First he breaks the conventional rules by waiting until the very end of the letter to say thank you. Then he writes as though he didn't really need the gift! *Read Philippians 4:10–23.*

1. What things does Paul find pleasing about the Philippians' gift?

2. Why is Paul so careful to let the Philippians know that he isn't dependent on their gift (vv. 11–13)?

3. What is Paul's "secret of being content" (v. 12)?

4. How did Paul learn this secret?

5. In what situations are you least likely to be content? How can Paul's secret be applied to your situation?

6. How had the Philippians helped Paul both in the past and the present (vv. 14–18)?

7. What opportunities do you have to meet the needs of those whose ministries require special support?

8. What benefits does Paul expect the Philippians to receive from their giving (vv. 17–19)?

9. How can the promise of verse 19 encourage us to give to the needs of others?

10. Many people complain that missionaries are always asking for money. How does this passage provide a model for both missionaries and those who support them?

11. How will this passage affect your giving?

Pray that God will use your gifts to meet the physical and emotional needs of his servants.

Now or Later

Take time to review what you have learned from your study of Philippians.

---

12. What are the major themes Paul has emphasized in Philippians?

---

13. What principles have you learned about living with meaning and purpose (1:20–26)?

about living with a proper attitude toward yourself and others (2:1–11)?

about the value of knowing Christ (3:4–11)?

about living a peaceful and contented life (4:4–19)?

---

14. What changes have you observed in your life as a result of studying Philippians?

Leader's Notes

MY GRACE IS SUFFICIENT FOR YOU. (2 COR 12:9)

Leading a Bible discussion can be an enjoyable and rewarding experience. But it can also be *scary*, especially if you've never done it before. If this is your feeling, you're in good company. When God asked Moses to lead the Israelites out of Egypt, he replied, "O Lord, please send someone else to do it!" (Ex 4:13). It was the same with Solomon, Jeremiah and Timothy, but God helped these people in spite of their weaknesses, and he will help you as well.

You don't need to be an expert on the Bible or a trained teacher to lead a Bible discussion. The idea behind these inductive studies is that the leader guides group members to discover for themselves what the Bible has to say. This method of learning will allow group members to remember much more of what is said than a lecture would.

These studies are designed to be led easily. As a matter of fact, the flow of questions through the passage, from observation to interpretation to application, is so natural that you may feel the studies lead themselves. This study guide is also flexible. You can use it with a variety of groups—student, professional, neighbourhood or church groups. Each study takes forty-five to sixty minutes in a group setting.

There are some important facts to know about group dynamics and encouraging discussion. The suggestions listed below should enable you to fulfil your role as leader effectively and enjoyably.

Preparing for the Study

1. Ask God to help you understand and apply the passage in your own life. Unless this happens, you will not be prepared to lead others. Pray too for the various members of the group. Ask God to open your hearts to the message of his Word and motivate you to action.

2. Read the introduction to the guide to get an overview of the entire book and the issues that will be explored.

3. As you begin each study, read and reread the assigned Bible passage to familiarize yourself with it.

4. This study guide is based on the New International Version of the Bible. It will help you and the group if you use this translation as the basis for your study and discussion.

5. Carefully work through each question in the study. Spend time in meditation and reflection as you consider how to respond.

6. Write your thoughts and responses in the space provided in the study guide. This will help you to express your understanding of the passage clearly.

7. It might help to have a Bible dictionary handy. Use it to look up any unfamiliar words, names or places. (For additional help on how to study a passage, see chapter five of *How to Lead a LifeBuilder Study*, IVP, 2018.)

8. Consider how you can apply the Scripture to your life. Remember that the group will follow your lead in responding to the studies. They will not go any deeper than you do.

9. Once you have finished your own study of the passage, familiarize yourself with the leader's notes for the study you are leading. These are designed to help you in several ways. First, they tell you the purpose the study guide author had in mind when writing the study. Take time to think through how the study questions work together to accomplish that purpose. Second, the notes provide you with additional background information or suggestions on group dynamics for various questions. This information can be useful if people have difficulty understanding or answering a question. Third, the leader's notes can alert you to potential problems you may encounter during the study.

10. If you wish to remind yourself of anything mentioned in the leader's notes, make a note to yourself below that question in the study.

Leading the Study

1. Begin the study on time. Open with prayer, asking God to help the group to understand and apply the passage.

2. Be sure that everyone in your group has a study guide. Encourage the group to prepare beforehand for each discussion by reading the introduction to the guide and by working through the questions in the study.

3. At the beginning of your first time together, explain that these studies are meant to be discussions, not lectures. Encourage the members of the group to participate. However, do not put pressure on those who may be hesitant to speak during the first few sessions. You may want to suggest the following guidelines to your group.

   • Stick to the topic being discussed.

   • Your responses should be based on the verses which are the focus of the discussion and not on outside authorities such as commentaries or speakers.

   • These studies focus on a particular passage of Scripture. Only rarely should you refer to other portions of the Bible. This allows for everyone to participate in in–depth study on equal ground.

   • Anything said in the group is considered confidential and will not be discussed outside the group unless specific permission is given to do so.

   • We will listen attentively to each other and provide time for each person present to talk.

   • We will pray for each other.

4. Have a group member read the introduction at the beginning of the discussion.

5. Every session begins with a group discussion question. The question or activity is meant to be used before the passage is read. The question introduces the theme of the study and encourages group members to begin to open up. Encourage as many members as possible to participate and be ready to get the discussion going with your own response.

This section is designed to reveal where our thoughts or feelings need to be transformed by Scripture. That is why it is especially important not to read the passage before the discussion question is asked. The passage will tend to color the honest reactions people would otherwise give because they are, of course, supposed to think the way the Bible does.

You may want to supplement the group discussion question with an ice-breaker to help people to get comfortable. See the community section of the *Small Group Starter Kit* (IVP, 1995).

You also might want to use the personal reflection question with your group. Either allow a time of silence for people to respond individually or discuss it together.

6. Have a group member (or members if the passage is long) read aloud the passage to be studied. Then give people several minutes to read the passage again silently so that they can take it all in.

7. Question 1 will generally be an overview question designed to briefly survey the passage. Encourage the group to do this, but try to avoid getting sidetracked by questions or issues that will be addressed later in the study.

8. As you ask the questions, keep in mind that they are designed to be used just as they are written. You may simply read them aloud, or you may prefer to express them in your own words.

   There may be times when it is appropriate to deviate from the study guide. For example, a question may have already been answered. If so, move on to the next. Or someone may raise an important question not covered in the guide. Take time to discuss it, but try to keep the group from going off at a tangent.

9. Avoid answering your own questions. If necessary, repeat or rephrase them until they are clearly understood, or point out something you have read in the leader's notes to clarify the context or meaning. An eager group quickly becomes passive and silent if they think the leader will do most of the talking.

10. Don't be afraid of silence. People may need time to think about the question before formulating their answers.

11. Don't be content with just one answer. Ask, "What do the rest of you think?" or "Anything else?" until several people have given answers to the question.

12. Acknowledge all contributions. Try to be affirming whenever possible. Never reject an answer. If it is clearly off-base, ask, "Which verse led you to that conclusion?" or again, "What do the rest of you think?"

13. Don't expect every answer to be addressed to you, even though this will probably happen at first. As group members become more at ease, they will begin to truly interact with each other. This is one sign of healthy discussion.

14. Don't be afraid of controversy. It can be very stimulating. If you don't resolve an issue completely, don't be frustrated. Move on and keep it in mind for later. A subsequent study may solve the problem.

15. Periodically summarize what the group has said about the passage. This helps to draw together the various ideas mentioned and gives continuity to

the study. But don't preach.

16. At the end of the Bible discussion you may want to allow group members a time of quiet to work on an idea under "Now or Later." Then discuss what you experienced. Or you may want to encourage group members to work on these ideas between meetings. Give an opportunity during the session to allow people to talk about what they are learning.

17. Conclude your time together with conversational prayer, adapting the prayer suggestion at the end of the study to your group. Ask for God's help in following through on the commitments you have made.

18. End on time.

Many more suggestions and helps are found in *How to Lead a LifeBuilder Study*.

Components of Small Groups

A healthy small group should do more than study the Bible. There are four components to consider as you structure your time together.

Nurture. Small groups help us to grow in our knowledge and love of God. Bible study is the key to making this happen and is the foundation of your small group.

Community. Small groups are a great place to develop deep friendships with other Christians. Allow time for informal interaction before and after each study. Plan activities and games that will help you get to know each other. Spend time having fun—going on a picnic or cooking dinner together.

Worship and prayer. Your study will be enhanced by spending time praising God together in prayer or song. Pray for each other's needs—and keep track of how God is answering prayer in your group. Ask God to help you apply what you are learning in your study

Outreach. Reaching out to others can be a practical way of applying what you are learning, and it will keep your group from becoming self-focused. Host a series of evangelistic discussions for your friends or neighbors. Clean up the yard of an elderly friend. Serve at a soup kitchen together, or spend a day working in the community.

Many more suggestions and helps in each of these areas are found in the *Small Group Starter Kit*. You will also find information on building a small group. Reading through the starter kit will be worth your time.

Study 1. Acts 16:6–34.
The God Who Pursues Us.

Purpose: To see how God begins the good work of salvation in us and then works together with his servants to complete it.

Question 2. For this question it would be helpful to obtain a large map of Paul's second missionary journey or to make copies of a map for each participant. Group members should be encouraged to identify on the map the places mentioned.

Verses 6–8 bring up the very interesting question of how the Holy Spirit prevented Paul and his companions from preaching in Asia and entering Bithynia. Unfortunately, the book of Acts doesn't give any clues. It could have been an inward prompting, a prophecy given by a Christian they encountered on the way or an external circumstance such as bad weather. Whatever the means, Paul saw it as clear guidance by the Holy Spirit.

E. M. Blaiklock makes this interesting observation:

> These regions where Paul was forbidden to preach were not passed by in the progress of the gospel. There is evidence of very early foundations in Mysia, and for Bithynia there is the evidence of Pliny's famous letters. This Roman governor, writing sixty years later, speaks of the grip which Christianity had secured over his province, and of the measures of repression undertaken by him. (*The Acts of the Apostles*, Eerdmans, 1959, p. 123.)

Question 3. F. F. Bruce explains that meeting Lydia at the river would have been natural given Paul's evangelistic style:

> When Paul visited a new city, it was his practice to attend the local Jewish synagogue on the first sabbath after his arrival and seek an opportunity there for making the message known "to the Jew first." At Philippi, however, there does not appear to have been a synagogue. That can only mean that there were very few Jews in the place: had there been ten Jewish men, they would have sufficed to constitute a synagogue. No number of women could compensate for the absence of even one man necessary to complete the quorum of ten. There was, however, an unofficial meeting–place outside the city where a number of women Jewesses and God–fearing Gentiles—came together to go through the appointed Jewish service of prayer for the sabbath day, even if they could not constitute a regular synagogue congregation. (*The Book of Acts*, Eerdmans, 1954, p. 331.)

Question 4. In his book *The Fight* John White says that there is no simple formula for knowing God's will.

Since you never know all the circumstances, you may sometimes have to ignore those you do know. Your gifts, usually, but not necessarily, have a bearing on your vocation. It is wise to seek advice, but sometimes you will have to go against it. Your inward desires may or may not point you in the direction God would have you go. Subjective sensations may represent the spirit leading or your own self–will. Only moral laws (yet only where they apply) serve as unchanging guides to conduct.

How then can you be guided?

It seems to me that what you need is not a formula but an attitude, an attitude with three related components:

1. You must share God's outlook;
2. You must will God's will; and
3. You must trust God.

(InterVarsityPress, 1976, p. 172.)

Question 6. The owners had no interest in the girl. She was being tormented by a demon, but the owners didn't care because the girl's torment was earning them money. Therefore, the owners could only understand this event from the perspective of how it affected them. They believed that they had been robbed of a valuable asset and could not see that God had worked a miracle, demonstrated his power, and was able to do great things in their lives as well.

Question 8. "Paul was in custody in the town jail, under the charge of a keeper, where there was an inner, perhaps underground, chamber containing stocks. These would have several holes, allowing the legs to be forced wide apart to ensure greater security and greater pain." (D. H. Wheaton, "Prison," in *New Bible Dictionary*, Eerdmans, 1962, p. 1035.)

Question 9. George Sweeting suggests, "Perhaps Paul and Silas did not know what else to do. Their plans for carrying out God's will seemed disrupted. Their itinerary did not include a stop at the Philippian jail; but in response to catastrophe they turned to God" (*The Acts of God*, Moody Press, 1986, p. 134).

Question 10. Verses 26 and 27 tell us that there was a "violent earthquake" and the prison's foundations were shaken. The jailer woke up to find the doors open and the prisoners' chains loose.

He was about to commit suicide (27), because he would have been held responsible, when Paul shouted to him not to harm himself because the prisoners were all there (28). Haenchen refers to this whole episode as "a nest of improbabilities", and so indeed it must appear to those who approach it with sceptical presuppositions. But the eye of faith, which believes in a gracious, sovereign God, sees the probabilities instead, as he works all things together for good. (John R.W. Stott, *The Message of Acts*, Nottingham: IVP, 1990, p. 267.)

Study 2. Philippians 1:1–11. An Encouraging Example.

Purpose: To help people strengthen their Christian relationships as they encourage each other with affirmation, godly affection and prayer.

Group discussion. Rather than going around the group in a circle, you could begin with the shortest person and work your way through the group by height.

Question 2. One of Paul's reasons for writing to the Philippians was to thank them for sending a gift of money to help him out while he was in prison. However, Paul is much more thankful for the people themselves and for the quality of their caring than he is for the money.

Question 3. Paul's statement in verse 6 takes on new meaning when we reflect on how the Philippian church was founded. This would be a good time to briefly review those things which God did in bringing the church into being. Alec Motyer states, "Christian assurance arises from observable facts providing evidence that these people are truly children of God" (*The Message of Philippians*, The Bible Speaks Today, IVP, 1984, p. 46).

Question 5. According to James M. Boice,

> In the first Christian century the world was filled with barriers, just as it is filled with barriers in our time, barriers of race, wealth, education, and culture. … Fellowship was found first and only among Christians. Christians were one. They confessed one Lord. They knew one salvation. All of the barriers of the empire were there within the Christian Church, but the Christians simply overlooked them. They met, not as antagonists, but as those who had been called out of darkness by Jesus Christ and made alive in Him. They loved one another. And the world marveled. One of the great pagan writers exclaimed, "Behold how these Christians love one another!" (*Philippians: An Expositional Commentary*, Zondervan, 1971, pp. 47–48.)

Question 6. According to Jac J. Muller, Paul's use of the term "partnership" in verse 5 includes many different aspects.

> Their acceptance of the gospel in faith, their identification with the aims thereof, their co-operation in preaching and spreading it, [and] their expression of sympathy with the apostle in his afflictions for the sake of Christ. … In short, it refers to their sympathetic attitude and practical

action in the interest of the gospel: their co-operation, zeal, prayers and sacrifice, arising from their personal appropriation of the gospel by faith. (*The Epistles of Paul to the Philippians and to Philemon*, Eerdmans, 1955, p. 41.)

Question 7. "In praying for the Christians at Philippi, Paul asks for three things. He prays that their love may abound in all knowledge and discernment. He prays that their lives might be free of hypocrisy. And he prays, looking forward to the natural result of the first two requests, that they might be filled with "the fruits of righteousness" (Boice, *Philippians*, p. 53).

Question 9. We know that for the Philippians life was rough (see 1:29–30). However, Paul does not tell them how to merely hold their ground during suffering but how to use the suffering to grow.

Study 3. Philippians 1:12–30. Joy in the Worst of Times.

Purpose: To help people follow Paul's example in dealing with adversity in a way that brings honor to Christ.

Question 1. Not only is Paul in prison, but his very life is at stake (1:20) and colleagues have turned against him (1:17). In the next chapter (2:2527) we will also learn that the person who was sent to help him became ill and had to go home.

Question 2. People are often amazed that Paul is able to be joyful in the midst of such difficult circumstances. If he were living merely for his own happiness and pleasure, then his joy would be senseless. But because he was living for Jesus Christ and the advancement of his kingdom, Paul had reason for joy: Jesus Christ was being preached and exalted because of Paul's imprisonment.

Question 3. The identity of those who "preach Christ out of envy and rivalry" (v. 15) is somewhat of a puzzle. Scholars seem to agree that they could not have been heretics who were taking advantage of Paul's imprisonment to teach false doctrine. Paul writes that he rejoices because "Christ is preached." If the preaching were heretical, Paul would never have made this statement. The envious preachers must have been Christians who personally disliked the apostle and hoped he would remain in prison. They probably saw the imprisonment as an opportunity to steal some of Paul's popularity and authority.

Question 4. Paul does not mean that our motives for preaching are unimportant. If Paul were writing to the envious preachers, he would certainly have sent a harsh message. But Paul is talking about himself and saying that what happens to him and his reputation doesn't matter as long as Christ is being promoted.

Question 6. Alec Motyer writes:

> As far as personal enrichment was concerned, death would win hands down. But there is also the Philippian church and all the others who fill the loving imagination of Paul. What of them? They still need (as he sees it) his apostolic ministry. Paul believes it to be the will of the Lord that this need should be considered paramount (verse 25). Furthermore, such is his love for his fellow-believers and his desire for their spiritual advantage that he is ready for it to be so. ... For him, it all came down to two dominating motives: I live on so that others may grow in Christ and that Christ may be glorified in me. (*Philippians*, p. 91.)

Question 8. The word translated as "conduct yourselves" means to "act as a citizen." James Boice explains why the use of this particular word is significant.

> Philippi enjoyed a privileged relationship to Rome. Prior to the great civil war in which Octavian finally defeated Antony, Philippi was like any other city in the empire. After the battle a number of soldiers who had been favorable to Antony were settled there. Because of this the city was given special prominence, and from this time on the town of Philippi became a Roman colony. This meant that as far as the courts were concerned Philippi became a part of Rome, even though it was nearly 800 miles away. The ground at Philippi became Italian soil. Citizens of the city became Romans. Roman law was practiced by the local civil administration. As far as possible the frontier city on the outer bounds of the empire adopted Roman customs. To be a colony was something of which any city in the empire was proud. Consequently, the Philippians took great delight in identifying themselves as Romans. ... All of this explains why Paul's phrase "to conduct oneself worthy of citizenship" is so significant. Paul knew how proud the Philippians were of their earthly citizenship. He knew that they allowed it to affect not only the laws of their city but also their social customs and the daily conduct of their lives. How much more then were they to be proud of their citizenship in heaven! This was the greater citizenship. They were to cherish it. They were to live by its laws and its customs. Moreover, they were to extend the influence of this commonwealth in the midst of a pagan and spiritually hostile environment. (*Philippians*, pp. 102–3.)

Question 11. This question is designed to help people relate Paul's example to their immediate circumstances. Be ready to model this for the group by sharing how you plan to face a specific difficulty. This discussion can very naturally lead into a time of prayer.

Study 4. Philippians 2:1–18. The Path of Humility.

Purpose: To discover how the humble service of Christ is an example for our Christian lives.

Question 1. If it is difficult for your group members to think of humanity as something demeaning, ask them to consider giving up their status as a human to become a dog. What would they find demeaning about this switch?

Question 2. These verses describe humility not as a way of looking at ourselves but as a way of relating to others with a readiness to serve them as people who are equally deserving of respect and honor.

Question 3. Jesus' humility is shown in what he willingly gave up. The phrase "did not consider equality with God something to be grasped" (v. 6) teaches that although he possessed the "very nature" of God, he did not demand his rights as God. Jesus could have appeared as the ruler of the universe instead of as its Savior, thereby receiving all the recognition that was due him. Instead, Jesus gave up all rights and came as a servant.

Question 6. God gave his own name and title to the Son. In doing this the unity and equality of the Father and the Son was proclaimed.

Question 7. Paul does not ask us to do anything for others that Christ has not already done for us (see v. 1). Christ's service to us is our motivation to do the same for others. God rewarded Christ's humility by exalting him in glory. It has been suggested that verses 14–16 teach that when we humble ourselves, God will also exalt us. What do you think?

Question 8. We can think of the words *work out* (v. 12) in the same way that we would work out in a gym. God has given us salvation. Now it is our job to exercise that salvation in the real world just as we should exercise the muscles God gave us. At the same time, God "works in" us to complete what he has begun.

Paul seems to use the phrase "with fear and trembling" (v. 12) to express a humble frame of mind. For other examples of this phrase see 1 Corinthians 2:3 and 2 Corinthians 7:15.

Question 10. Some members of your group may be uncomfortable with the word boast. It is true that some versions substitute proud, but the force of the Greek is much stronger than this. Consider Webster's definition of boast: "to glory in having or doing something."

Study 5. Philippians 2:19–30. Servants of Christ.

Purpose: To be spurred to acts of Christian service by looking at the examples of the lives of Timothy, Epaphroditus, Paul and the Philippians.

Group discussion. No artistic talent is needed for this project. Simple drawings and stick figures depicting character qualities or events will be sufficient. An alternative to drawing could be making a collage from magazine pictures.

Question 2. Timothy is being sent as Paul's envoy and representative. His mission will be a powerful follow-up to the concerns of Paul's letter.

Questions 4–5. These questions combine interpretation and application. Before the group can properly answer question 4, they must think about the needs of the church: What are Christ's interests and concerns for the church? How might Timothy have demonstrated his concern for the welfare of the church? Question 5 then helps the group to think about how they might follow Timothy's example in their own church or fellowship group.

Question 6. Why was Epaphroditus homesick? Some scholars believe that he was a leader in the Philippian church and felt a pastoral responsibility for his congregation. Others suggest that he yearned to stand beside his brothers and sisters through a time of persecution. Paul was afraid that Epaphroditus might be criticized for returning and that the Philippians might conclude their mis-sion had failed. Therefore Paul clearly states that the return was his idea. Paul also gives a glowing commendation of Epaphroditus to put a stop to any criti-cism. Epaphroditus was to be welcomed back with joy and honor as a missionary who had completed his task. The exact nature of his sickness is a mystery.

Question 8. Epaphroditus should be honored because the example he set in humility, sacrifice and service reflected the humility of Jesus Christ (2:6–8). The honor that the Philippians give to their servant Epaphroditus will reflect the honor God gave to his servant, Jesus Christ (2:9–11).

Question 9. Your group may want to write a thank you note to a staff worker, pastor, missionary or other leader as a way of showing that person honor. Or you might honor the person with a party, phone call or special event.

Study 6. Philippians 3:1–11. Rejoice in the Lord.

Purpose: To show that while our attempts at self-righteousness cause distress, accepting Christ's righteousness through faith brings rejoicing.

Question 1. In this passage Paul describes the misery he felt when he tried to live a righteous life, knowing that he could never be good enough. This misery is contrasted with the joy of understanding grace and having the Lord rule over his life and destiny.

Question 3. The people Paul is describing were known as "Judaizers" and believed all Christians should live strictly by the Jewish laws and customs. Notice how Paul satirically calls these people "dogs" in verse 2. Dogs was a derogatory title used by orthodox Jews to describe Gentiles, whom they saw as God's enemies. By this change in terms Paul points out that it is the Judaizers and not the Gentiles who are God's enemies. "Mutilators of the flesh" refers to the Jewish law of circumcision.

Question 5. Paul says that all of our attempts to live a righteous life are like a circumcision that only cuts the skin and doesn't reach the heart. There is a big difference between acting righteous and being righteous. We might be successful at making ourselves look righteous, but if our hearts have not been changed by Christ, then it is only a show.

Question 6. Answers to this question will vary depending on your group and the religious background of your members, but it may include pressure to dress in a particular way, attend certain meetings, vote for the right candidates, speak in tongues or avoid speaking in tongues.

Question 8. Paul has undergone a revaluing of all his values. Jac J. Muller writes:

> The things that were gain to him, the carnal advantages and privileges in which he put confidence—religion, race and descent, law–observance, zeal and outward blamelessness—are now, for the sake of Christ, regarded as loss and even harm, as a result of the absolute transformation his life had undergone. Christ made all the difference. The things he formerly cherished as valuable, appeared not only worthless, but even harmful. "It is not Nil that takes the place of the former Plus, but the Plus itself is changed to a Minus" (Barth). In the light of Christ Paul sees the guilt, wrong and rejectableness of the supposed "irreproachable life" of Pharisaic righteousness, and how it endangered the soul's salvation. (*Epistles of Paul*, pp. 112–13.)

Question 10. The group will probably need help with this question, since verses 10–11 are difficult to interpret.

"The power of his resurrection" does not just refer to the power that raised Christ from the dead. It also refers to the power of the resurrected Christ, who is at work in the life of every believer.

"The fellowship of sharing in his sufferings" does not mean that Paul's suffering would somehow complete the atoning work of Christ. Yet Paul realized that every true follower of Jesus would experience suffering. Jesus said, "If they persecuted me, they will persecute you also" (Jn 15:20).

Paul's desire was also to become "like him in his death." Tradition tells us that Paul did experience martyrdom outside Rome. But every Christian is to take up his or her cross and follow Jesus, whether it results in death or not.

Verse 11 in some translations gives the impression that Paul was uncertain whether or not he would be raised from the dead. Instead of "if possible" (RSV) the NIV has "somehow," which better captures Paul's meaning. He is not uncertain about his own resurrection but rather the events leading to it.

Study 7. Philippians 3:12–4:1. Onward to the Goal.

Purpose: To consider what goals we have set for our lives and whether these goals are leading us toward heaven.

Question 1. Scholars disagree as to whom Paul is talking about in these verses. Some believe he is referring to the Judaizers mentioned earlier in the chapter (see note on study 6, question 3). Others believe he is talking about a group of Gentiles who insisted on living as they please. Although it may seem as if no two groups could be further apart, they are both guilty of the same thing— their heart is set on worldly things.

Question 2. Some commentators have suggested that Paul is describing a chariot race in these verses. J. A. Thompson writes:

> It seems like a picture of a chariot driver bent over the curved rail against which he presses his knees; the reins are round his body and stretching over the horse's back, and he leans his whole weight against them. A glance back would be fatal. So, says Paul, the Christian is to press on towards the end of the race of life, where a prize awaits him in heaven. (*Handbook of Life in Bible Times*, InterVarsity Press, 1986, p. 263.)

Question 3. Jac J. Muller gives us this insight into Paul's thinking:

> The recollections of what he was in his former unconverted state must not paralyze and discourage him; disappointments and temptations of the past must not depress him; the thought of what God had already done for him and through him must not lead him to slackness and self-satisfaction. The hand is put to the plough and he will not look back. (*Epistles of Paul*, p. 124).

Questions 6–7. Some of the people who were opposing Paul (the Gnostics) claimed that they had attained spiritual perfection so that it no longer mattered what their bodies did. They believed that their perfection gave them the freedom to live licentiously. Paul first claims that he is not yet perfect (v. 12) and then claims that he is perfect (the same Greek word is translated as both "mature" and "perfect"). Paul is probably using the term ironically. Even so, Paul does have the confidence that he is speaking as an apostle. He knew that he was right and his critics were wrong. Alec Motyer explains:

> The New Testament teaches the uniqueness of the apostolic band. Since the days of Paul and his fellow apostles, no–one has been able to say, "Am I not an apostle? Have I not seen Jesus our Lord?" No-one has been able to say, "The gospel which was preached by me … came through a revelation of Jesus Christ." No-one has been able to say, "Be imitators of me, as I am of Jesus Christ." The apostolic band had the unique, unrepeatable position of church-founders. They were organs of revelation, infallible teachers. But they were also—as here in the case of Paul—divinely-given examples of the way to live the life of Christ in the world. The church today is apostolic, not by virtue of any man or order of men claiming to be apostolic, but by virtue of its adherence to apostolic doctrine and its imitation of apostolic life as enshrined in and taught by the Scriptures. (*Philippians*, p. 180.)

Question 8. The enemies have denied the cross for themselves. Since they refuse to "take up the cross" and follow Jesus, they are now living for themselves.

Question 10. Paul has encouraged us to press on without looking back (vv. 12–13), keep our eyes on the prize (v. 14), listen to the truth from God (v. 15), live a godly life dedicated to the goal (vv. 16–17), remember our true citizenship (v. 20) and eagerly await Christ's return (v. 20).

Study 8. Philippians 4:2–9. Stress–free Living.

Purpose: To identify practices that have added stress to our lives and our Christian communities and to eliminate that stress through trust in God.

Question 2. Women were apparently quite influential in the Philippian church. We know from Acts 16 that the first convert was a woman. From this passage we learn that Euodia and Syntyche had worked at Paul's side in proclaiming the gospel. Therefore the quarrel between these women was all the worse because of their influence on others. Paul does not reveal what Euodia and Syntyche were disagreeing about, and he does not tell us who was at fault. For Paul the horror of the situation was not what had been said or done but that the unity of the church had been broken. His hope is that these women will humble themselves and give unity in the church priority over proving themselves right.

Question 3. A yokefellow is a companion or partner. It is unclear whom Paul is referring to as "loyal yokefellow." Some suggest that Paul is talking to someone who knows he has this gift and responsibility. Others believe that *syzygos* (Greek for "yokefellow") is a proper name which just happens to be very fitting. A third option is that Paul is putting out a general call for someone to take the role of yokefellow.

Question 5. Paul's appeals to joy are not simple encouragements to "look on the bright side." He tells us to rejoice "in the Lord." This phrase throws us back on our Lord who has protected us in the past and has the power to deliver us in the future.

Question 6. Ralph Martin says this exhortation to gentleness is "a call which prevents the church from being too preoccupied with its own interests; it is also a reminder that the church's setting in the world should summon it to a life of winsome influence on its pagan neighbors. Forbearance is a disposition of gentleness and fairmindedness to other people in spite of their faults, and inspired by the confidence Christians have that after earthly suffering will come heavenly glory" (*Philippians*, pp. 154–55).

Question 7. According to Alec Motyer:

> The antidote to anxiety, and the prelude to the enjoyment of peace, are to be found in the linked exercise of prayer and thanksgiving. In prayer, anxiety is resolved by trust in God. That which causes the anxiety is brought to the One who is totally competent and in whose hands the matter may be left. In thanksgiving, anxiety is resolved by the deliberate acceptance of the worrying circumstances as something which an all-wise, all-loving and all-sovereign God has appointed. Prayer takes up the anxiety-provoking question "How?"—How shall I cope?—and answers by pointing away to him, to his resources and promises. Thanksgiving addresses itself to the worrying question "Why?"— Why has this happened to me?—and answers by pointing to the great Doer of all who never acts purposelessly and whose purposes never fail. (*Philippians*, p. 211.)

Question 9. When we give our attention to the things of which God approves, our minds will be shaped to be like his.

Study 9. Philippians 4:10–23. A Guide for Giving.

Purpose: To see how giving benefits us and to be prompted to greater support of giving, especially to missions.

Question 2. Paul wanted to make it clear that he was not greedy for money, as some of his critics claimed. He also wanted people to understand that he was not dependent on human intervention. God would take care of him either through the Philippians or in some other way. Paul was called to preach and would continue to do so whether he received a stipend or not.

Question 3. The Stoic philosophers of Paul's time taught that people must be self-sufficient and find happiness by being content with their present lot, no matter what it is. Paul borrows from this philosophy but denies that we can find the resources to face life and death within ourselves.

> Paul finds the secret of life in his union with Christ (1:21) ... He can, therefore, proceed in the following section to declare that true liberty is his as he depends on God and is committed in obedience to a new Lord (v. 13). His freedom also disengages him from dependence on human resources, as though he were a hired worker of the church. (Martin, *Philippians*, p. 162)

Question 4. When members of the Greek mystery religions "learned a secret," they meant that they had worked their way up through the lower degrees and had finally received "the mystery" itself. Paul's knowledge came through a similar maturing process as he learned through his life experiences to trust God more and more completely. "Contentment is the mark of a mature believer, and an objective to be cultivated by all believers who want to grow in Christ" (Motyer, *Philippians*, p. 218).

Question 6. The Philippians sent money to Paul on at least three occasions: when he was preaching in Thessalonica (Phil 4:16), when he was in Corinth (2 Cor 11:9), and while he was in prison.

Question 8. "The gift to Paul obtains a greater worth and a higher significance when seen as an offering brought to God. What was given toward Paul's needs was sacrificed to God himself" (Muller, *Epistles of Paul*, p. 151).

The benefits to the Philippians are that they met their goal of supplying God's missionary, they performed an action which pleased God, and they were assured that God would meet their needs.

> God has promised to fill the need of the believer in Jesus Christ out of his infinite wealth and resources. He will expand us as time goes on, and we shall come to hold more. We shall become more and more like Jesus Christ. But even at the greatest extent of our enlarged capacity we shall only touch his resources slightly. And there will always be infinite resources beyond the ones we then experience. (Boice, *Philippians*, p. 298.)

Question 10. Paul wants the Philippians to know that his dependence is on God alone. Too often people think of missionaries as charity cases who are unable to make it on their own. With this attitude, missions–giving becomes an act of pity rather than what it really is—an investment in God's kingdom.

Now or Later. After studying each passage in its individual context, your group needs to step back and see how the major themes flow through the book. The purpose of this study is to tie together the themes of Philippians. Group members should be reminded of the issues they have confronted and leave with the feeling, "Now I know what Philippians is about and how it applies to my life." You may want to take a separate session to cover this review study.

Donald Baker, a former staff member with InterVarsity Christian Fellowship, is pastor of First Reformed Church of Doon, Iowa and Bethel Reformed Church of Lester, Iowa. He is also the author of the LifeBuilder Bible Studies *Joshua* and *Judges* and *1 & 2 Thessalonians*.